RUSTIC REVIVAL: DIY BARN AND FARMHOUSE RENOVATION TECHNIQUES

D.R. T Stephens

S.D.N Publishing

Copyright © 2023 S.D.N Publishing

All rights reserved

The characters and events portrayed in this book are fictitious. Any similarity to real persons, living or dead, is coincidental and not intended by the author.

No part of this book may be reproduced, or stored in a retrieval system, or transmitted in any form or by any means, electronic, mechanical, photocopying, recording, or otherwise, without express written permission of the publisher.

ISBN: 9798854879972

Cover design by: Art Painter
Library of Congress Control Number: 2018675309
Printed in the United States of America

CONTENTS

Title Page
Copyright
General Disclaimer — 1
Chapter 1: The Charm of Barn and Farmhouse Renovations — 3
Chapter 2: Getting Started: Planning Your Renovation — 5
Chapter 3: The Nitty-Gritty: Understanding Basic Carpentry — 8
Chapter 4: Essential Tools for Barn and Farmhouse Renovation — 11
Chapter 5: The Structure: Assessing the Bones of Your Building — 14
Chapter 6: Going Green: Eco-Friendly Renovation Tips — 17
Chapter 7: Roof Repair: A DIY Guide — 20
Chapter 8: Wall Renovation: From Patching to Painting — 22
Chapter 9: From The Ground Up: Floor Renovation Techniques — 24
Chapter 10: The Heart of the Home: Kitchen Renovation Ideas — 26
Chapter 11: DIY Bathroom Renovations: Creating a Modern Rustic Look — 29
Chapter 12: Bringing Life to Living Spaces — 32
Chapter 13: Reclaiming and Refurbishing: DIY Furniture Restoration — 34

Now, what should your plan include? Start with your end goal. Are you renovating your barn into a cozy living space, or are you refurbishing your farmhouse to its former glory? Your goal will determine the extent of your renovation and the tasks involved.

Next, assess your budget. Renovation, as rewarding as it is, can quickly become a costly endeavor. It's essential to have a realistic understanding of how much you're willing and able to spend. Remember, your budget should account not only for materials and equipment but also for unexpected expenses that inevitably arise during the renovation process.

Once you have your goal and budget sorted out, it's time to roll up your sleeves and delve into the specifics. List down all the tasks that need to be done. Start with major structural work like fixing the roof or replacing the floor, then move on to smaller tasks like painting the walls or refurbishing the furniture. Prioritize these tasks based on necessity, budget, and your overall timeline.

Speaking of timelines, it's vital to set a realistic one. Renovation is a marathon, not a sprint. It involves a lot of hard work, patience, and, let's be honest, a fair bit of sweat. Give yourself ample time for each task, considering potential delays due to weather, availability of materials, or unexpected issues that might crop up.

Lastly, don't forget to check local building codes and regulations before you start your renovation. Each area has its own rules regarding structural modifications, safety standards, and other renovation-related matters. Ensuring your project complies with these regulations will prevent you from any conceivable legal issues down the line.

So, there you have it, the blueprint to kickstart your renovation journey. Remember, the success of your project lies as much in the strength of your plan as it does in the swing of your hammer. Happy planning!

CHAPTER 3: THE NITTY-GRITTY: UNDERSTANDING BASIC CARPENTRY

Gather round, aspiring renovators! It's time to delve into the core of any DIY project: Carpentry. You might be thinking, "I'm not a carpenter; I'm a renovation enthusiast!" True, but if we are to embark on a barn or farmhouse renovation, a solid understanding of basic carpentry is not a suggestion; it's a requirement. It's the DIY-er's rite of passage, a test of tenacity, and often, a test of patience. But fear not! With a little knowledge and a healthy sprinkle of a can-do attitude, carpentry can become an enjoyable part of the DIY experience.

So, what is carpentry? In essence, it's the art and craft of cutting, shaping, and installing building materials, primarily wood. It's about transforming a pile of planks into a sturdy structure or a beautiful piece of furniture. It's both a practical skill and a creative endeavor.

Now, let's start with some basics: Understanding the wood. Not all woods are created equal. Some are harder, some softer; some are suitable for outdoors, others are best kept indoors. For most renovation projects, you'll likely encounter softwoods like pine or fir or hardwoods like oak or maple. Softwoods are generally simpler to work with and less expensive, while hardwoods are more durable but harder to cut and shape. Know the characteristics of the wood you're working with, and choose the type that best suits your needs and budget.

Next, let's talk about the tools of the trade. Every carpenter, amateur or professional, needs a well-stocked toolbox. Some must-haves include a reliable hammer, a set of screwdrivers, a good handsaw or circular saw, a measuring tape, a level, and a set of chisels. Don't forget safety equipment, too: goggles, gloves, and ear protection. Purchasing quality tools will not only make your job simpler but also safer and more enjoyable.

Measurements are the backbone of any carpentry project. When considering the measuring and marking of your wood for cuts, precision is key. A millimeter off here or there might not seem much, but it can lead to problems later on. Remember the old carpenter's adage, "Measure twice, cut once." It's not just a catchy phrase—it's a lifesaving mantra in the world of DIY.

Finally, understanding different types of cuts and joints is fundamental. From simple crosscuts and rip cuts to more complex dovetail and mortise and tenon joints, the type of cut or joint you use will depend on the project at hand. Basic carpentry books or online resources can be a great help in understanding these techniques.

Carpentry can seem a little daunting at first, but like any skill, it gets easier with practice. Start small, perhaps by building a simple piece of furniture or fixing a broken step, and gradually take on more complex projects. Before you know it, you'll be handling a jigsaw like a pro and referring to planks as 'stock.' Welcome to the world of carpentry! It's a place of endless creation, occasional frustration, and immense satisfaction. So, pick up that hammer, and let's get to it!

CHAPTER 4: ESSENTIAL TOOLS FOR BARN AND FARMHOUSE RENOVATION

Welcome to the toolbox tour! If you're anything like me, you might find a strange satisfaction in the heft of a well-made hammer or the sharp precision of a brand-new chisel. Perhaps it's the promise of transformation they hold or simply the raw, tactile pleasure of a tool well used. Either way, as any experienced DIY-er knows, the right tool can mean the difference between a job well done and, well, a barn that's still a bit too rustic.

So, what are these crucial implements that every barn and farmhouse renovator should have at their disposal? Let's take a look.

Hammer: A carpenter's best friend. Good for driving in nails, pulling them out, and occasionally (very occasionally) as an impromptu lever. I recommend a 16-ounce claw hammer for its balance of weight and utility.

Screwdrivers: A set of these in various sizes is essential. They're not just for screws—you'd be surprised at how often you'll find yourself using them for odd jobs like prying up floorboards or scraping off old paint.

Power Drill: A cordless drill can be a real game changer in a renovation project. Not only can it drill holes and drive screws much faster than you can manually, but with a set of different attachments, it can also sand, stir paint, and even cut holes.

Hand Saw & Circular Saw: For your cutting needs. A hand saw is perfect for smaller jobs, while a circular saw can make short work of bigger tasks like cutting plywood sheets or thick planks.

Tape Measure: Accuracy is key in renovation work, and a good tape measure is essential for this. Go for a 25-footer with a wide, sturdy tape.

Level: To ensure your work is plumb and level. This tool can save you from wonky shelves and crooked framing.

Pliers & Wrench Set: For everything from twisting wires to tightening nuts and bolts.

Safety Gear: Last but not least, your safety gear. This should include a pair of safety goggles, work gloves, and ear protection. Don't skimp on these—no renovation project is worth risking your health.

This is just a starter kit, of course. Depending on your project, you might need more specialized tools, like a miter saw for angled cuts, a jigsaw for curved or intricate cuts, a table saw for large quantities of lumber, or a sander for smoothing down rough surfaces.

And let's not forget ladders and scaffolding for reaching those high spots safely or a decent set of paintbrushes for that final, transformative coat of color.

Remember, your tools are an investment. Quality tools may have a higher upfront cost, but they'll pay dividends in the long run in terms of performance and durability. Look after them, and they'll look after you.

So, there you have it: the essential toolbox for any budding barn and farmhouse renovator. With these tools in hand, you're well on your way to transforming your rustic dreams into a reality. So, let's get out there, roll up our sleeves, and show that old building some love!

CHAPTER 5: THE STRUCTURE: ASSESSING THE BONES OF YOUR BUILDING

Every great masterpiece begins with a blank canvas—or in the case of barn and farmhouse renovations, a sturdy structure. Before we dive into the world of wall patching, floor polishing, and roof repairing, we need to get to grips with the bones of your building. Yes, indeed, it's time to put on our detective hats and dive into the exciting realm of structural assessments!

A structural assessment, to put it simply, is a thorough inspection to evaluate the state of your property's framework. Its goal is to ensure that your barn or farmhouse is solid, safe, and ready for renovation.

Let's break down the primary elements you'll need to assess:

1. Foundations: They are, quite literally, the base of your renovation. A weakened or damaged foundation can lead to significant issues down the line, including sloping floors, cracked

walls, and, worst-case scenario, structural failure. You'll want to check for visible signs of damage like cracks, uneven settling, or moisture issues.

2. Framing: This is the skeleton that holds your property together, typically made up of beams, posts, and joists. Pay special attention to signs of wood rot, insect damage, or any warping, cracking, or splitting in the beams.

3. Roof Structure: Not just the shingles—the underlying structure that supports them, including rafters and trusses. Look for sagging areas, water damage, and, again, any signs of rot or insect damage.

4. Walls: Examine both the interior and exterior walls for cracks, bowing, or movement. A good trick for checking if a wall is plumb is to roll a marble along it—if it veers off, you might have a problem.

5. Floor Structure: Check your floors for sloping, sagging, or bouncing. Soft spots can indicate rot or water damage.

Performing a thorough structural assessment is not just about identifying potential problems; it's also an opportunity to become intimately acquainted with your building. You'll get to know every nook and cranny, every beam and joist that contributes to the unique character of your property.

Of course, it's essential to mention that while DIY assessments can give you a good sense of your building's structural integrity, it's always a good idea to get a professional evaluation, especially for more significant issues like foundation problems. Remember, we're after rustic charm, not risky collapses.

And what do you do if you find a problem? Don't panic! Many structural issues can be repaired, and, indeed, the process of overcoming these hurdles is part of the rewarding journey of restoration. If you are unsure, consult a professional to guide you through the possible solutions.

Performing a structural assessment may seem like a daunting task. Still, it's an absolutely vital part of the renovation process, providing a solid (pun intended) foundation for all your future work. So, here's to sturdy beams, sound roofs, and solid floors – the unsung heroes of the renovation world!

CHAPTER 6: GOING GREEN: ECO-FRIENDLY RENOVATION TIPS

As we embark on our barn and farmhouse renovation journey, it's essential to remember that we're not just stewards of these historic structures but also of the planet we all call home. Yes, dear renovator, we're stepping into the verdant territory of eco-friendly renovation tips!

1. Resource Efficiency: The first step in a green renovation is understanding that every resource matters. By reusing and repurposing old materials, you're not only preserving the rustic charm of your barn or farmhouse, but you're also reducing the need for new materials, thus minimizing waste. So, before you throw away that old door, window, or beam, take a moment to ponder: Could it serve a new purpose?

2. Insulation: An often-overlooked hero in the eco-friendly game, proper insulation can significantly reduce energy consumption, keeping your home cozy in the winter months and cool in the summer. Using sustainable insulation materials like wool or cellulose can further increase the green quotient of your renovation.

3. Natural Light: Utilizing natural light is an excellent way to conserve energy and create inviting spaces. During your renovation, consider expanding window spaces or adding skylights to harness the power of the sun. Remember, natural light isn't just green; it's also flattering!

4. Energy-Efficient Appliances: When you're renovating rooms like the kitchen or bathroom, choosing energy-efficient appliances may save you a considerable amount of money by make a massive reduction in your overall energy usage. Look for appliances with an Energy Star rating—your wallet and the planet will thank you.

5. Sustainable Materials: When you need new materials for your renovation, aim for sustainability. Choose local, recycled, or sustainably sourced materials whenever possible. Not only do they have a lower carbon footprint, but they also often come with a story—adding a little extra charm to your rustic revival.

6. Water Conservation: The use of water-saving fixtures, rainwater harvesting systems, and native, drought-resistant plants for landscaping can all contribute to a significant reduction in water usage. Every drop counts!

Remember, going green doesn't mean sacrificing style or comfort. On the contrary, many eco-friendly practices enhance the rustic charm of your barn or farmhouse. It's about creating a home that's not only comfortable and beautiful but also respectful of the environment.

So, embrace the eco-friendly adventure, renovators! Here's to creating homes that are as kind to the environment as they are pleasing to the eye. After all, the greenest building is the one that's already built, and with a little care and creativity, it can be a model of sustainable living.

CHAPTER 7: ROOF REPAIR: A DIY GUIDE

There's an old saying among the rustic revivalists: "If the roof ain't right, neither's the rest." But worry not, fellow renovators, tackling a roof repair isn't as intimidating as it sounds, and this guide will walk you through the process, one shingle at a time.

1. Assess the Situation: Before rushing to replace every tile and timber, it's crucial to assess the situation. Start by looking for signs of damage, both from inside your barn or farmhouse and from the outside. Water stains, mold, missing or damaged shingles—all of these are telltale signs that your roof needs some TLC.

2. Get Your Materials: Once you've identified the problem areas, it's time to gather your materials. Depending on the type and extent of the damage, you might need replacement shingles or tiles, roofing nails, sealant, and a sturdy ladder. Always prioritize safety gear, including a helmet and harness. Remember, a good renovator is a safe renovator!

3. Replace Damaged Shingles: Damaged shingles are typically easy to spot and replace. Start by carefully removing the damaged shingle along with any nails. Slide the new shingle into place, align it with the surrounding ones, and secure it with roofing nails. Apply a bit of roof sealant around the nail heads for an extra

layer of protection.

4. Fix Leaks: Fixing leaks may require a bit more detective work. Begin by locating the source point for the leak from inside the attic, then trace it to the corresponding spot on the roof. From there, the process is typically the same as replacing a shingle. If the leak persists, don't hesitate to call a professional—it's always better to be safe than soggy!

5. Regular Maintenance: Like any aspect of home renovation, roofs benefit from regular maintenance. Keep an eye out for potential issues such as moss growth, which can cause shingles to lift, or loose flashing, the metal pieces used to prevent water from seeping into intersections of the roof.

Roof repair can seem daunting, especially given its crucial role in protecting your home. But with the right knowledge, tools, and a good dose of DIY spirit, it's a task that can certainly be managed. Just remember to prioritize safety and know when to call in the experts.

So, dust off your work gloves and don your hard hat because, with these tips, you're well on your way to becoming the lord or lady of your own (well-maintained) manor! And remember, no renovation is too big or small when you're armed with knowledge and a can-do attitude. As they say, keep calm and roof on!

CHAPTER 8: WALL RENOVATION: FROM PATCHING TO PAINTING

If your barn or farmhouse walls could talk, they would probably tell you tales of hard work, resilience, and the changing seasons. But over time, these rustic charmers may have collected more than just stories—they may also have collected wear, tear, and quite possibly, a whole host of other structural and aesthetic issues. But have no fear; this guide is here to take you from patching to painting with good humor and easy-to-follow steps.

1. Inspecting and Assessing: First things first, take a good look at your walls. What are they telling you? Are there holes, cracks, or water damage? Or perhaps they're just a little worn around the edges? Whatever it may be, a keen eye and careful inspection are the first steps in any renovation project.

2. Patching and Repair: Once you've identified the areas that need attention, it's time to get to work. For small holes and cracks, a quick patch-up with some filler or plaster will do the trick. However, larger holes or extensive water damage may require replacing sections of the wall. Don't forget to sand the area down after patching to ensure a smooth finish.

3. Preparing for Painting: Now, onto the fun part—painting! But hold on, let's not get ahead of ourselves. Correct preparation is vital to a successful paint job. Start by cleaning the walls to remove any dirt or dust, then apply a primer. Priming is important as it ensures that the paint adheres well to the surface of the wall and also delivers a consistent base for your chosen color.

4. Painting: Now it's time to let your artistic side shine. When painting, start from the top and work your way down, using a roller for larger sections and a brush for all the corners and edges. Remember, two thin coats of paint are generally better than one thick one, but only if you enable the first coat time to dry completely before applying the second.

5. The Finishing Touches: Lastly, consider the finishing touches. Perhaps a rustic faux finish to give the room some character? Or how about some wall stencils for that farmhouse chic vibe? The sky—or rather, the wall—is the limit!

Throughout this process, remember that renovation is as much an art as it is a science. There's room for creativity, mistakes, and do-overs. So, put on some old clothes, crank up your favorite tunes, and dive into the world of wall renovation.

And if you're ever feeling overwhelmed, just think of every patch, every brush stroke, every new piece of wall as a chapter in your barn or farmhouse's ongoing story—a story that you're now a part of. Happy renovating!

CHAPTER 9: FROM THE GROUND UP: FLOOR RENOVATION TECHNIQUES

Flooring is more than just a surface to walk on—it sets the tone for your home and plays a critical role in displaying its character. If your barn or farmhouse floor has seen better days, a little TLC can help breathe new life into it. In this chapter, we'll take you step by step through the process of floor renovation, turning that old barn floor into a charming, rustic surface that ties together your revived homestead.

1. Assessing the Situation: Begin with a thorough examination of your existing floor. Is it structurally sound, or are there issues like rot, sagging or insect damage? If you discover structural problems, these will need to be addressed before moving on to aesthetics.

2. Choosing Your Material: Next, you'll need to choose a material that suits both the character of your home and your personal style. Reclaimed wood offers a rich, rustic feel that's perfectly at home in a barn or farmhouse. On the other hand, stone or tile can provide an appealing contrast and are particularly suited to kitchens and bathrooms.

3. Prep Work: Before you begin laying your new floor, you'll need to prepare the surface. This means ensuring it's clean, level, and free of any debris. If you're installing wood flooring, you'll also want to let the wood acclimate to your home's humidity level to prevent warping or shrinking after installation.

4. Installation: Now, the fun part: laying your new floor! Each material will have its own unique installation process. For example, with wood flooring, you'll start at the longest wall and move across the room, staggering the ends of the boards for a natural look.

5. Finishing Touches: Depending on your chosen material, you might finish with a sealant, polish, or a coat of varnish. This not only enhances the look of your floor but also helps protect it from wear and tear. Just imagine the satisfaction of seeing your new floor shine under a fresh coat of polish—it's almost like the cherry on top of a labor of love!

6. Maintenance and Care: Finally, keep your renovated floor looking its best with regular care. This will vary depending on your chosen material but could involve regular sweeping, mopping, or the occasional reseal or polish.

Remember, your floor is the base upon which you'll build your beautifully renovated barn or farmhouse. It's the grounding element that ties everything else together, so taking the time to install it right is well worth the effort. Just think of it as laying down the foundation for all the good times to be had in your revived home. So, let's roll up those sleeves and get started—it's time to build from the ground up!

CHAPTER 10: THE HEART OF THE HOME: KITCHEN RENOVATION IDEAS

The kitchen is more than just a place where meals are prepared. It's the heart of the home, a gathering spot for family and friends, and a place where memories are made. This chapter will provide you with ideas and strategies to transform your barn or farmhouse kitchen into a rustic yet functional space that exudes warmth and hospitality.

1. Assessing the Space: Before you dive into the renovation, consider the current state of your kitchen. Take into account the available space, the layout, and any existing features you want to preserve. This step is crucial in establishing a plan that matches your vision and the practical needs of your daily life.

2. Setting a Theme: A cohesive theme can unify your kitchen's design. In a rustic farmhouse, you might opt for elements such as exposed wooden beams, antique fixtures, and distressed cabinetry. Alternatively, you might want to blend rustic charm with modern convenience, incorporating elements such as stainless steel appliances amidst the rustic setting.

3. Cabinets and Countertops: Choosing the right cabinets and countertops can significantly affect the look and feel of your kitchen. Reclaimed wood cabinets can add a hearty dash of rustic charm, while stone countertops, such as granite or soapstone, can provide a durable and attractive preparation surface.

4. Flooring and Walls: As we explored in the previous chapter, flooring plays a crucial role in defining the character of a space. Consider materials like wide-planked wood or natural stone for a truly rustic feel. For the walls, a whitewash or light paint can make the space feel brighter and larger, while exposed brick or stone can add a cozy, vintage touch.

5. Lighting: The right lighting can make your kitchen come alive. For a rustic feel, consider vintage-style pendant lights, lanterns, or a chandelier made from antlers or wrought iron. Don't forget about natural light, too – consider enlarging existing windows or adding a skylight to flood your kitchen with sunlight.

6. Modern Appliances with a Vintage Twist: While you want to keep the rustic charm, you also want a functional kitchen. Look for modern appliances that have a vintage aesthetic. Many brands offer appliances that combine the latest technology with a design that echoes the past.

7. Finishing Touches: Personal touches can transform a renovated kitchen into a comfortable, lived-in space. Hang pots and pans on a rustic overhead rack; add an antique wooden table for casual meals, or decorate the walls with vintage signs or farm tools.

Renovating your kitchen is a journey, so remember to enjoy the process. With each step, you're crafting a space that isn't just about cooking but about living. In a renovated farmhouse or barn, the kitchen truly is the heart of the home. And like any heart, it thrives on warmth, love, and a touch of that rustic charm that makes it all so uniquely yours.

CHAPTER 11: DIY BATHROOM RENOVATIONS: CREATING A MODERN RUSTIC LOOK

When renovating your barn or farmhouse, your attention is likely to be drawn to high-traffic areas like the kitchen or the living room. However, a well-designed, comfortable bathroom can be a sanctuary in your home, a place to relax and refresh. This chapter will take you through the process of creating a modern rustic bathroom that harmoniously blends comfort, function, and charm.

1. Plan Your Space: Before any renovation, it's crucial to assess the available space. Measure the bathroom accurately, taking into account door and window positions. Consider your needs and wants: Do you dream of a claw-foot tub under a rustic wooden beam or a walk-in shower with natural stone tiles?

2. Choose Your Style: Rustic doesn't have to mean antiquated. A modern rustic look combines the charm and texture of natural, reclaimed materials with the sleek lines and functionality

of modern design. Exposed wood, stone sinks, and vintage accessories can live harmoniously with stainless steel faucets, modern lighting, and eco-friendly technologies.

3. Bathtub and Shower: The shower or tub is often a focal point in the bathroom. For a rustic touch, consider a freestanding copper bathtub or a stone-walled shower. Use vintage-style fixtures to enhance the look.

4. Vanity and Sink: A reclaimed wood vanity can add immense character to your bathroom. Top it with a vessel sink made of copper or stone for a striking rustic look. Pair it with modern faucets and hardware to bring in a touch of the contemporary.

5. Flooring: Consider using materials that evoke a rustic feel but stand up to water, such as stone or distressed wood tiles. Heated flooring can be a great addition for those cold mornings – a little touch of modern luxury in your rustic oasis.

6. Lighting: Good lighting is vital in a bathroom. Consider a mix of modern and rustic light sources – overhead lighting for functionality, wall sconces for a touch of elegance, and perhaps a vintage chandelier for a bit of whimsy.

7. Storage: In a rustic bathroom, storage should be as charming as it is practical. Consider open shelving made from reclaimed barn wood or vintage baskets and crates for a creative and attractive way to store your essentials.

8. Finishing Touches: This is where you can really let your personality shine. Add a rustic ladder towel rack, vintage mirrors, or antique metal hooks. Even everyday items like soap dispensers can be an opportunity to add a touch of rustic charm.

Renovating a bathroom might seem like a daunting task, but with careful planning, a clear vision, and a modicum of creativity, you can devise a modern rustic bathroom that offers comfort, functionality, and that oh-so-cozy rustic charm. Remember, your home is a reflection of your journey, and every plank, stone, or tile you place in your renovation is a part of the story you are telling. So, roll up your sleeves, pick up your tools, and let's bring that vision to life!

CHAPTER 12: BRINGING LIFE TO LIVING SPACES

Living spaces form the heart of a home; they're where we gather, celebrate, relax, and live our daily lives. When you're renovating your rustic property, it's essential to create living spaces that are not only functional but also comfortable and full of character. Here's how you can transform your living areas into spaces that truly feel like home.

1. Celebrate the Architecture: Rustic properties often come with architectural details like exposed beams, brick walls, and vaulted ceilings. Rather than covering these features, celebrate them. For example, highlighting an exposed brick wall with strategic lighting can create a stunning focal point in your living room.

2. Choose the Right Furniture: Choose furniture that suits the scale of your space and aligns with your rustic aesthetic. Don't shy away from pieces with a bit of history. An antique wooden table or a weathered leather sofa can add instant character to a room.

3. Lighting Matters: A well-lit room feels warm and inviting. Utilize a combination of ambient, task, and accent lighting to achieve the right balance. Consider fixtures that enhance

your rustic style—wrought iron chandeliers, vintage sconces, or lamps with Edison bulbs can all contribute to a warm, rustic atmosphere.

4. Go Natural: Incorporate natural materials wherever possible. Use wood, stone, leather, wool, and cotton in your furniture, flooring, and décor. They bring warmth and texture to your interiors and are hallmarks of rustic style.

5. Define Areas with Rugs: In large, open-plan living spaces, area rugs can help define different zones, such as a sitting area, a reading nook, or a dining space. Select rugs that are produced from natural materials like wool or jute, and don't be afraid to layer them for an added sense of coziness and depth.

6. Bring in the Green: Plants breathe life into any room. Larger potted plants can serve as focal points, while smaller plants make great accents on tables and shelves. Choose easy-to-care-for varieties that thrive in your home's light conditions.

7. Add Personal Touches: Finally, remember that your living spaces are just that—yours. Display items that hold meaning for you. Family photos, travel souvenirs, a cherished book collection, or heirloom pieces can all serve to personalize your space.

Rustic doesn't mean outdated or uncomfortable. By thoughtfully choosing your furnishings and décor and by preserving and celebrating the unique features of your property, you can create living spaces that marry rustic charm and modern comfort. As you work on your living spaces, remember that they are meant to be lived in—don't strive for magazine perfection. Instead, aim for spaces that invite you in, tell your story, and make you want to put your feet up and stay awhile.

CHAPTER 13: RECLAIMING AND REFURBISHING: DIY FURNITURE RESTORATION

Embarking on a renovation journey often means discovering neglected or worn-out furniture pieces that are just aching for a second life. Perhaps you've unearthed an old farmhouse table in the barn or a vintage armoire tucked away in the attic. These pieces, with their character and history, can become central elements of your rustic home design. So, deep breath, roll up your sleeves, grab your tools, and let's dive into the art of DIY furniture restoration.

1. Assess the Piece: The first step in any restoration project is to thoroughly assess the piece. Check for damage, such as cracks, loose joints, or signs of wood rot. Consider the extent of the restoration needed - is it a minor cosmetic job, or does the piece require more extensive structural repairs?

2. Gather Your Tools: Essential tools for furniture restoration include sandpaper, wood glue, clamps, a paintbrush, and

depending on the condition of your furniture, possibly wood filler or a putty knife. Of course, safety goggles and gloves are a must.

3. Prep and Clean: Start by cleaning the piece to remove dust, grime, or old peeling paint. A soft cloth and warm soapy water usually do the trick. Once clean, allow the piece to dry completely.

4. Sand and Repair: Use sandpaper to remove the old finish and smooth out rough areas. Start with coarse-grit sandpaper and gradually move to finer grits for a smooth finish. For any cracks or holes, use wood filler to repair them. Remember to let the filler dry and then sand it down to level with the rest of the surface.

5. Finish it Off: Now, it's time to finish your piece. You could stain it to highlight the natural grain of the wood or paint it for a fresh, new look. Always remember to apply a sealant like a varnish or wax to protect the piece and give it a lovely sheen.

6. Reupholster If Needed: If you're dealing with chairs or other upholstered items, you may need to replace the old, worn-out fabric. Choose a sturdy fabric that complements your rustic design. Basic sewing skills and a staple gun are usually enough for a DIY reupholstering project.

Restoring furniture is not just about saving money; it's also about reclaiming a piece of history and reducing waste. So next time you come across a neglected piece of furniture, don't be quick to discard it. With a little bit of hard work and creativity, you will be able to transform it into a statement piece that adds a touch of rustic charm to your newly renovated barn or farmhouse. Just remember, the key to successful furniture restoration is patience – good things, as they say, take time.

CHAPTER 14: THE OUTSIDE COUNTS: REVIVING YOUR EXTERIOR AND LANDSCAPING

As the saying goes, you'll never get a second chance to make a first impression. While the inside of your home is the heart of your living space, the exterior and landscape often provide that crucial first impression to visitors and even to yourself after a long day. This chapter will guide you through breathing life back into the outdoor areas of your rustic property, from the walls to the walkways and beyond.

1. Exterior Assessment: To start, assess the current condition of the exterior. Are there any damages to the siding, windows, or doors? Is the paint peeling? What is the condition of the porch or patio? Your assessment should extend to the landscaping. Are there overgrown shrubs, underutilized spaces, or erosion issues that need attention?

2. Prepping the Exterior: Depending on the materials used for your exterior, the preparation can range from a good wash to

patching holes, sanding, and applying primer. Always remember safety first - use a sturdy ladder when necessary and always have someone spot you.

3. Choosing Your Paint: When choosing exterior paint, consider the weather conditions your home will endure and the material of your exterior. Most importantly, choose a color that complements the natural surroundings and fits the rustic aesthetic. Try earthy hues like warm browns, sage greens, or soft blues to blend harmoniously with the landscape.

4. The Greenery: A well-landscaped yard can transform the look of your property. Select specific plants that are native to your region for a more sustainable garden that's easier to maintain. Don't forget to add a few trees for shade and consider installing raised garden beds for a charming farmhouse touch.

5. Paving the Way: Walkways and driveways should be inviting and practical. Gravel, brick, and stone are great rustic options that offer good drainage and can endure heavy wear. Remember to ensure your pathways are wide enough for comfortable passage and that they lead your visitors naturally toward the entrance.

6. Adding Personal Touches: Lastly, consider personal touches like a rustic wooden bench, a swing hanging from a sturdy tree, or a garden sculpture to add personality to your outdoor space. You could also install outdoor lighting to illuminate your walkways at night and create a welcoming glow from your windows.

Reviving the exterior and landscaping of your property requires thoughtful planning, a bit of elbow grease, and a healthy dose of creativity. But remember, Rome wasn't built in a day, and your rustic oasis won't be either. Take your time to create an outdoor space that complements the charm and character of your barn or farmhouse. Happy renovating!

CHAPTER 15: PRESERVING CHARACTER: WORKING WITH ORIGINAL FEATURES

You might have fallen in love with your rustic property because of its character. Maybe it was the original barn doors, the worn wooden beams, or the quirky hardware on the farmhouse cabinets. This chapter is all about preserving those distinctive features that give your property its unique rustic charm.

1. Recognizing Value in Originality: Original features often have a lot more to offer than just aesthetics. They can give your property a sense of history, authenticity, and uniqueness that new, modern replacements may lack. They can also be a fascinating window into how people lived when your home was first built.

2. Assessment and Evaluation: First, you need to decide which features are worth preserving and which might need to go. Some original features may not be up to modern safety standards or may be too damaged to repair. Enlist the help of a professional if you're unsure. Remember, this isn't about stubbornly keeping

everything old—it's about preserving the charm while creating a safe and comfortable home.

3. Repair or Replace: Next, figure out whether the feature needs repairing or replacing. Is the old barn door just weather-worn, or is it falling apart? An antique expert or experienced carpenter can help you determine the best course of action.

4. The Gentle Touch: When you're working with original features, always start with the least invasive procedure. For instance, start cleaning wooden beams with a gentle soap before moving to stronger wood cleaners. Remember, you can always do more, but it's hard to undo overzealous cleaning or repair attempts!

5. Embracing the Quirks: No old barn or farmhouse is without its quirks. Maybe it's a crooked beam or a stained glass window in an odd place. Instead of seeing these as flaws to be corrected, embrace them as part of your property's unique charm.

6. Integrate and Adapt: Finally, consider how you can integrate original features into your renovation plans. Could the barn loft be transformed into a cozy bedroom with its exposed beams? Could the old weather vane be a focal point in your landscaping? A bit of creative thinking can bring old features to life in new ways.

Preserving the character of your property is about more than just retaining original features. It's about respecting and celebrating its history while ensuring it meets the needs of the present. And while not every original feature will be salvageable, those you can save will infuse your home with a depth and character that's uniquely yours. Happy renovating!

CHAPTER 16: SAFETY FIRST: BARN AND FARMHOUSE RENOVATION SAFETY TIPS

Now, you're fully immersed in the process of rustic revival, but let's hit the pause button for a moment and focus on a crucial aspect of any renovation project: safety. As much as we adore the excitement of transforming old into new, it's essential that the adventure doesn't turn into a misadventure. So, let's venture into the realm of safety protocols without losing our charm, of course.

1. The Safety Gear Collection: Always start your renovation work fully armed with safety gear. It's not quite the latest fashion trend, but a sturdy helmet, safety goggles, gloves, and steel-toe boots can become your best friends on the renovation battlefield.

2. Old House, New Hazards: Old barns and farmhouses can hide a multitude of hazards. Lead-based paint, asbestos insulation, mold, and unstable structures are common issues. If you suspect these problems, do call in professionals. After all, bravery has its limits!

3. Tool Time: Your tools are the magic wands of your renovation fairy tale, but they can also be the villains if not handled correctly. Always follow the manufacturer's guidelines when using tools, especially power ones, and ensure they are kept clean and well-maintained. A rusty saw is more 'tetanus nightmare' than a 'rustic revival'!

4. The Power of Electricity: Working around electricity demands caution. Before you start any renovation, ensure the electrical supply is off, especially when dealing with old and potentially faulty wiring. Engage a qualified electrician for complex electrical work - no one likes a shocking experience, do they?

5. Ladder Logic: Ladders are the unsung heroes of any renovation, but a wobbly one can rapidly turn from friend to foe. Always ensure your ladder is stable and in good condition before embarking on your ascent to DIY glory.

6. First Aid Fundamentals: Despite all precautions, accidents may happen. So, always keep a well-stocked first aid kit nearby. And, of course, in case of serious injuries, don't hesitate to call for medical help.

7. Respect the Dust: This might sound odd, but dust can be more harmful than you'd think. Old homes can generate dust containing harmful substances. So, use dust masks and maintain good ventilation during your renovation work.

8. Rest, Relax, Repeat: Renovation work can be physically demanding. Remember to take regular breaks, hydrate, and listen to your body. You are the project's most valuable tool, after all.

Safety might not be the most glamorous part of a renovation, but it's undeniably the most essential. By putting safety first, you can ensure your barn or farmhouse transformation is a joyous journey, not a perilous plight. Happy and safe renovating!

CHAPTER 17: DIY VS. PROFESSIONAL HELP: KNOWING WHEN TO CALL IN EXPERTS

We all love the romantic idea of being a true DIYer—just you, a hammer, a barn full of potential, and the open skies. It's a picture as old as barns themselves. But even the most ruggedly independent renovator needs a helping hand now and then. In this chapter, we'll decipher the puzzle of when to put on the tool belt and when to hang it up and dial the pros.

1. Structural Evaluation: While you've learned to assess the "bones" of your building, determining the soundness of the foundation and structural supports often calls for an expert eye. Structural engineers can analyze the integrity of these elements, helping to prevent any house of cards scenarios.

2. Electrical Work: Some electrical tasks, like replacing a light fixture, can be done with a little DIY spirit. But rewiring or dealing with an old, possibly non-compliant, electrical system is not the place for amateur experiments. So, it's often best to let the certified electricians take the lead on this.

3. Plumbing: Replacing a faucet? Go for it. Repiping your entire home or installing a new bathroom from scratch? You might want to dial a plumber. The potential for costly mistakes is high, and there are often codes and regulations to consider.

4. Roofing: While basic roof repairs can be a DIY project, large-scale roof replacement is best left to the professionals. Aside from the technicalities, there's a serious safety factor to consider here.

5. Asbestos and Lead: If your rustic beauty was built before the 1980s, it might have asbestos or lead-based paint. Both can be harmful if disturbed, and their safe removal requires specialized knowledge and equipment.

6. HVAC Systems: Installing a new heating, ventilation, and air conditioning (HVAC) system is not an ideal DIY project. It requires specialized knowledge, and an improperly installed system can lead to efficiency issues and increased costs.

So, when the DIY path seems more like an uphill struggle, don't feel defeated! Even the most hardcore DIYer needs to call in the pros occasionally. Remember, renovation is a symphony, and sometimes you need more than one instrument to make beautiful music. By knowing when to tackle a job yourself and when to call in the cavalry, you're guaranteed a smoother renovation experience and a safer, sounder end result.

CHAPTER 18: UPCYCLING AND REPURPOSING: CREATIVE DIY PROJECTS

Welcome to the world of upcycling and repurposing, where old items are given a second life, and waste is a thing of the past. By the end of this chapter, you'll view everything around you as a canvas for your creativity!

1. Barn Wood Wall Art: Not all old wood has to be discarded during renovations. With a bit of cleaning, sanding, and sealing, your barn wood can be transformed into an impressive piece of wall art. Let the rustic texture and grain of the wood be the star, and create a geometric pattern for an added touch of modern design.

2. Pallet Furniture: With a bit of elbow grease and imagination, old pallets can be transformed into functional furniture, such as coffee tables, bookshelves, or even a wine rack. A piece of sanded and varnished pallet furniture in your living room or kitchen adds a bespoke, rustic touch to your decor.

3. Reclaimed Window Frames: Repurpose old windows as a quirky photo frame or a chalkboard for your kitchen. You could even add a mirror behind them for a unique vintage touch.

4. Farm Tool Decor: Have some old farm tools lying around? An old pitchfork could become a coat hanger, or an antique plow could double as a unique wall decoration. This is a fun way to honor your barn's past while adding a splash of rustic charm to your home.

5. Old Door Table: An old door can be an excellent foundation for a DIY dining table or desk. With some sturdy legs and a glass top, you can create a one-of-a-kind table that tells a story.

6. Rustic Chandeliers: Old wagon wheels, mason jars, or even barn wood can be transformed into an eye-catching rustic chandelier. Hang it in your living room or dining area for an instant touch of farmhouse chic.

7. Salvaged Wood Shelves: Whether they're displaying your favorite books or treasured family photos, shelves made from salvaged wood are both practical and aesthetically pleasing.

The magic of upcycling and repurposing lies in the joy of giving old objects a new lease on life and, in the process, adding personality and warmth to your barn or farmhouse. So, don your thinking cap, roll up your sleeves, and let the repurposing revolution begin! After all, one man's trash is another man's treasure, especially when that man is a savvy DIY renovator.

CHAPTER 19: CASE STUDIES: SUCCESSFUL BARN AND FARMHOUSE RENOVATIONS

A picture may be worth a thousand words, but a good case study can tell a whole story. Let's delve into a few successful barn and farmhouse renovations that have transformed these rustic buildings into inviting and cozy homes. Remember, these examples are here to inspire and motivate you, not to be copied exactly. Each rustic revival is as unique as its renovator!

1. The Heritage Haven: This 1920s farmhouse in rural Kansas was suffering from years of neglect before the Johnson family embarked on their renovation journey. Their aim was to honor the history of the home, so they chose to preserve as many original features as possible, including the claw-foot tub and original timber beams. But they didn't shy away from modern upgrades. Solar panels were integrated into the design, and a modern, energy-efficient HVAC system was installed. The blend of old-world charm with 21st-century convenience makes this property a true heritage haven.

2. The Barn Loft: When the Smiths took on a dilapidated barn in upstate New York, they saw potential in the ample space. They transformed the hayloft into a second-story living area complete with repurposed barn wood floors, a modern kitchen, and floor-to-ceiling windows that overlooked their sprawling property. By creatively utilizing the existing space, the Smiths were able to maintain the barn's original structure while adapting it to their needs.

3. The Eco Farmhouse: In Oregon, the Williams couple converted an old farmhouse into a model of eco-friendly living. They installed a rainwater harvesting system, utilized recycled materials throughout the renovation, and upcycled old furniture into new pieces. The result was a rustic, environmentally-conscious home that served as a testament to the Williams' commitment to sustainable living.

4. The Cozy Cottage: This 1930s farmhouse in North Carolina was given a new lease of life by the Thompson family. They focused on creating a cozy and warm atmosphere by exposing the original brick fireplace, installing reclaimed hardwood flooring, and using a muted, calming color palette throughout the home.

These successful renovations are examples of how creativity, patience, and hard work can turn an old, rundown building into a dream home. Whether your focus is preserving history, environmental sustainability, or simply creating a cozy retreat, there is a world of possibility in every old barn and farmhouse. Just remember, the beauty of a rustic revival lies in its unique reflection of your vision and personality. Let these success stories be your inspiration, but don't be afraid to carve your own path!

CHAPTER 20: SELLING YOUR HOME: IMPACT OF RENOVATIONS ON PROPERTY VALUE

When it comes to property, the saying 'You have to spend money to make money' could not be more apt. By investing time, money, and hard work into your barn or farmhouse renovation, you could significantly increase its market value. But it's crucial to remember not all renovations are created equal in the eyes of prospective buyers and property appraisers. So, let's delve into how to make the most of your rustic revival for a profitable sale.

The Renovation Value Proposition: The beauty of barn and farmhouse renovations is that they offer a unique charm that newly-built houses can't quite replicate. This rustic allure, coupled with thoughtful renovations, can increase your home's desirability and, consequently, its market value. It's a simple equation, really - the more appealing your property is to potential buyers, the more they're willing to pay for it.

Quality Over Quantity: Here's a key piece of advice. Go for quality over quantity. While adding an extra bathroom or extending the kitchen could boost the property's value, a poorly executed renovation will do just the opposite. The craftsmanship and materials used in your renovation play a big role in determining the added value.

Eco-Friendly Upgrades: Green renovations aren't just good for the planet; they're good for your wallet too. Home improvements like solar panels, energy-efficient appliances, and good insulation can increase the property's value, and they often appeal to eco-conscious buyers.

Maintaining Original Features: The unique character of old barns and farmhouses often lies in their original features. Preserving elements like exposed beams, original fireplaces, or even the old barn door can increase the charm factor and the property's value.

Curb Appeal: Don't underestimate the power of a good first impression. The exterior of your property is the first thing potential buyers will see, so reviving the external appearance and landscaping can significantly increase your property's value.

Professional Appraisal: Once your renovation project is complete, consider getting a professional appraisal. An appraiser will look at your renovations, the overall state of the property, and comparable homes in your area to give you a good estimate of your property's current market value.

When you decide to sell your renovated barn or farmhouse, remember to highlight the improvements and unique features in the listing. Buyers appreciate knowing the story behind a property, especially when it's one of rustic revival, sweat, and possibly a few happy tears.

In essence, renovations can have a substantial impact on your property's value, but the key lies in planning and executing them thoughtfully. By investing in quality workmanship, preserving original character, and going green, you can ensure that your renovated property isn't just a labor of love but also a smart financial investment.

CHAPTER 21: CONCLUSION: CELEBRATING THE BEAUTY OF RUSTIC LIVING

Throughout this book, we have traveled a long and winding road, from dusty barns and neglected farmhouses to beautifully renovated rustic homes. But beyond the technical details and the step-by-step guides, what truly matters is the experience and the resulting charm of your property that makes it more than just a building. It's the celebration of a lifestyle, a testament to the beauty of rustic living.

The rustic living style is about simplicity, warmth, and harmony with nature. In our fast-paced world, these homes serve as sanctuaries, echoing the tranquility of country life. Whether it's the weathered wood, the exposed brickwork, or the repurposed furniture, every detail has a story to tell. It speaks of a time gone by and breathes character into the home.

Renovating a barn or farmhouse is not just about beautification or adding value to a property. It's also about preserving heritage and breathing new life into something that has been forgotten. Through this renovation journey, you've brought back a piece of history, maintaining a connection with the past while making it suitable for modern living.

The scent of freshly cut wood, the creaking of old floorboards, the satisfaction of seeing your handiwork come alive—these experiences are unique to the rustic revival journey. The journey might be filled with splinters and dust, but the joy of seeing a neglected space transform into a beautiful and functional home is unparalleled.

Renovation is not a finite process but a continuous journey of maintaining and improving your home. Now that you've mastered barn and farmhouse renovation techniques, perhaps you'll find a new project to embark upon—a shed, a loft, or maybe a vintage camper for some rustic adventures on wheels.

Through all this, remember your home is a reflection of you. It is your canvas to paint the colors of your soul. Whether you decide to live in it, rent it out, or sell it for a tidy profit, your renovated property is more than a structure of bricks and wood. It's a symbol of your creativity, hard work, and love for rustic charm.

In conclusion, embrace the beautiful chaos that comes with DIY renovation. Celebrate each small victory, learn from the challenges, and enjoy the process. Here's to the rustic revival, to the preservation of charming old buildings, and to the amazing DIYer in you who makes it all possible. So, roll up those sleeves, strap on your tool belt, and keep that DIY spirit alive. The world of rustic renovation is waiting for you!

CHAPTER 22: YOUR NEXT PROJECT: KEEPING THE DIY SPIRIT ALIVE

As we pull down the rustic barn door on this book, don't think for a moment that we're saying goodbye. If anything, this is just the beginning of your do-it-yourself adventure. Whether you have just completed your first project or are already an old hand, remember that the world of DIY barn and farmhouse renovations is as expansive as a country skyline. There's always something new to learn, a different technique to try, another project to start.

The first rule of DIY club is - don't stop DIY-ing! The beautiful thing about this journey is that each project equips you with a new skill set, a newfound confidence, and an evolved perspective that will make your next project even better. Did you find a particular joy in restoring old furniture? Maybe next time, you could focus on creating custom pieces from scratch. Found the green renovation techniques intriguing? Why not delve deeper into eco-friendly living and try installing a solar energy system? The possibilities are endless!

A key aspect of keeping the DIY spirit alive is staying curious. Continually explore new ideas, materials, and methods.

Magazines, online resources, and communities of like-minded DIYers can be a treasure trove of inspiration. Stay updated, participate in forums, ask questions, share your experiences, and learn from others.

Always keep an eye out for potential projects. That dilapidated garden shed at your cousin's place? It could become an enviable 'she-shed' or 'he-shed.' Or maybe you have some leftover wood from your renovation? How about building a rustic picnic table for the backyard? Once you start viewing the world through DIY-tinted glasses, you'll realize that opportunities for creativity are everywhere.

However, in this pursuit of the next project, don't forget to appreciate the journey as much as the destination. After all, DIY is as much about the process as it is about the end result. It's about those moments of problem-solving, the pride in your work, the bonding with family and friends over a shared project, and yes, even the inevitable hiccups that make for funny stories later on.

Lastly, share your love for DIY. Pass on the knowledge you've acquired, and encourage others to try their hand at it. There's something truly satisfying about being part of someone else's DIY journey, about helping them discover the joy of creating something with their own hands.

In the end, the goal isn't just to renovate barns and farmhouses. It's about cultivating creativity, resourcefulness, patience, and a certain can-do spirit that goes beyond renovations. It's about creating homes that are not just beautiful but also imbued with memories and love. It's about embracing the essence of the rustic lifestyle - the charm of simplicity, the warmth of the familiar, and the beauty of nature.

So, as you close this book, don't let it be an end. Let it be the spark that ignites a lifetime of DIY adventures. Strap on your tool belt, my friend, and let's keep the rustic revival alive. To your next project, and the many more to follow - may they be as exciting and fulfilling as the journey we've embarked on together in "Rustic Revival: DIY Barn and Farmhouse Renovation Techniques."

THE END

Printed in Great Britain
by Amazon